THE ESSENTIAL NOTE KEEPING
CHEMISTRY LAB BOOK
FOR STUDENTS

Activinotes

DAILY JOURNALS, PLANNERS, NOTEBOOKS AND OTHER BLANK BOOKS

_____

Student's Name

_____

Chemistry Class/ Teacher

_____

Contact

_____

Email Address

TITLE		BOOK No.	DATE
NAME		PROJECT No.	FROM PAGE No.

SIGNATURE	DATE	WITNESS/INSTRUCTOR	DATE

Date: _____

TITLE:

INTRODUCTION:

MATERIALS AND METHODS:

PROCEDURES:

GRAPHS OR TABLES

SUMMARY:

CALCULATIONS

FORMULAS

TITLE		BOOK No.	DATE
NAME		PROJECT No.	FROM PAGE No.

SIGNATURE	DATE	WITNESS/INSTRUCTOR	DATE

Date: _____

TITLE:

INTRODUCTION:

MATERIALS AND METHODS:

PROCEDURES:

GRAPHS OR TABLES

SUMMARY:

CALCULATIONS

FORMULAS

TITLE	BOOK No.	DATE
NAME	PROJECT No.	FROM PAGE No.

SIGNATURE	DATE	WITNESS/INSTRUCTOR	DATE

Date: _____

TITLE:

INTRODUCTION:

MATERIALS AND METHODS:

PROCEDURES:

GRAPHS OR TABLES

SUMMARY:

CALCULATIONS

FORMULAS

TITLE	BOOK No.	DATE
NAME	PROJECT No.	FROM PAGE No.

SIGNATURE	DATE	WITNESS/INSTRUCTOR	DATE

Date: _____

TITLE:

INTRODUCTION:

MATERIALS AND METHODS:

PROCEDURES:

GRAPHS OR TABLES

SUMMARY:

CALCULATIONS

FORMULAS

TITLE		BOOK No.	DATE
NAME		PROJECT No.	FROM PAGE No.

SIGNATURE	DATE	WITNESS/INSTRUCTOR	DATE

Date: _____

TITLE:

INTRODUCTION:

MATERIALS AND METHODS:

PROCEDURES:

GRAPHS OR TABLES

SUMMARY:

CALCULATIONS

FORMULAS

TITLE	BOOK No.	DATE
NAME	PROJECT No.	FROM PAGE No.

SIGNATURE	DATE	WITNESS/INSTRUCTOR	DATE

Date: _____

TITLE:

INTRODUCTION:

MATERIALS AND METHODS:

PROCEDURES:

GRAPHS OR TABLES

SUMMARY:

CALCULATIONS

FORMULAS

TITLE	BOOK No.	DATE
NAME	PROJECT No.	FROM PAGE No.

SIGNATURE	DATE	WITNESS/INSTRUCTOR	DATE

Date: _____

TITLE:

INTRODUCTION:

MATERIALS AND METHODS:

PROCEDURES:

GRAPHS OR TABLES

SUMMARY:

CALCULATIONS

FORMULAS

TITLE		BOOK No.	DATE
NAME		PROJECT No.	FROM PAGE No.

SIGNATURE	DATE	WITNESS/INSTRUCTOR	DATE

Date: _____

TITLE:

INTRODUCTION:

MATERIALS AND METHODS:

PROCEDURES:

GRAPHS OR TABLES

SUMMARY:

CALCULATIONS

FORMULAS

TITLE	BOOK No.	DATE
NAME	PROJECT No.	FROM PAGE No.

SIGNATURE	DATE	WITNESS/INSTRUCTOR	DATE

Date: _____

TITLE:

INTRODUCTION:

MATERIALS AND METHODS:

PROCEDURES:

GRAPHS OR TABLES

<u>SUMMARY:</u>

<u>CALCULATIONS</u>

<u>FORMULAS</u>

TITLE	BOOK No.	DATE
NAME	PROJECT No.	FROM PAGE No.

SIGNATURE	DATE	WITNESS/INSTRUCTOR	DATE

Date: _____

TITLE:

INTRODUCTION:

MATERIALS AND METHODS:

PROCEDURES:

GRAPHS OR TABLES

SUMMARY:

CALCULATIONS

FORMULAS

TITLE	BOOK No.	DATE
NAME	PROJECT No.	FROM PAGE No.

SIGNATURE	DATE	WITNESS/INSTRUCTOR	DATE

Date: _____

TITLE:

INTRODUCTION:

MATERIALS AND METHODS:

PROCEDURES:

GRAPHS OR TABLES

SUMMARY:

CALCULATIONS

FORMULAS

TITLE		BOOK No.	DATE
NAME		PROJECT No.	FROM PAGE No.

SIGNATURE	DATE	WITNESS/INSTRUCTOR	DATE

Date: _____

TITLE:

INTRODUCTION:

MATERIALS AND METHODS:

PROCEDURES:

GRAPHS OR TABLES

SUMMARY:

CALCULATIONS

FORMULAS

TITLE		BOOK No.	DATE
NAME		PROJECT No.	FROM PAGE No.

SIGNATURE	DATE	WITNESS/INSTRUCTOR	DATE

Date: _____

TITLE:

INTRODUCTION:

MATERIALS AND METHODS:

PROCEDURES:

GRAPHS OR TABLES

SUMMARY:

CALCULATIONS

FORMULAS

TITLE	BOOK No.	DATE
NAME	PROJECT No.	FROM PAGE No.

SIGNATURE	DATE	WITNESS/INSTRUCTOR	DATE

Date: _____

TITLE:

INTRODUCTION:

MATERIALS AND METHODS:

PROCEDURES:

GRAPHS OR TABLES

SUMMARY:

CALCULATIONS

FORMULAS

TITLE	BOOK No.	DATE
NAME	PROJECT No.	FROM PAGE No.

SIGNATURE	DATE	WITNESS/INSTRUCTOR	DATE

Date: _____

TITLE:

INTRODUCTION:

MATERIALS AND METHODS:

PROCEDURES:

GRAPHS OR TABLES

SUMMARY:

CALCULATIONS

FORMULAS

TITLE		BOOK No.	DATE
NAME		PROJECT No.	FROM PAGE No.

SIGNATURE	DATE	WITNESS/INSTRUCTOR	DATE

Date: _____

TITLE:

INTRODUCTION:

MATERIALS AND METHODS:

PROCEDURES:

GRAPHS OR TABLES

SUMMARY:

CALCULATIONS

FORMULAS

TITLE		BOOK No.	DATE
NAME		PROJECT No.	FROM PAGE No.

SIGNATURE	DATE	WITNESS/INSTRUCTOR	DATE

Date: _____

TITLE:

INTRODUCTION:

MATERIALS AND METHODS:

PROCEDURES:

GRAPHS OR TABLES

SUMMARY:

CALCULATIONS

FORMULAS

TITLE		BOOK No.	DATE
NAME		PROJECT No.	FROM PAGE No.

SIGNATURE	DATE	WITNESS/INSTRUCTOR	DATE

Date: _____

TITLE:

INTRODUCTION:

MATERIALS AND METHODS:

PROCEDURES:

GRAPHS OR TABLES

SUMMARY:

CALCULATIONS

FORMULAS

TITLE	BOOK No.	DATE
NAME	PROJECT No.	FROM PAGE No.

SIGNATURE	DATE	WITNESS/INSTRUCTOR	DATE

Date: _____

TITLE:

INTRODUCTION:

MATERIALS AND METHODS:

PROCEDURES:

GRAPHS OR TABLES

SUMMARY:

CALCULATIONS

FORMULAS

TITLE	BOOK No.	DATE
NAME	PROJECT No.	FROM PAGE No.

SIGNATURE	DATE	WITNESS/INSTRUCTOR	DATE

Date: _____

TITLE:

INTRODUCTION:

MATERIALS AND METHODS:

PROCEDURES:

GRAPHS OR TABLES

SUMMARY:

CALCULATIONS

FORMULAS

TITLE	BOOK No.	DATE
NAME	PROJECT No.	FROM PAGE No.

SIGNATURE	DATE	WITNESS/INSTRUCTOR	DATE

Date: _____

TITLE:

INTRODUCTION:

MATERIALS AND METHODS:

PROCEDURES:

GRAPHS OR TABLES

SUMMARY:

CALCULATIONS

FORMULAS

TITLE		BOOK No.	DATE
NAME		PROJECT No.	FROM PAGE No.

SIGNATURE	DATE	WITNESS/INSTRUCTOR	DATE

Date: _____

TITLE:

INTRODUCTION:

MATERIALS AND METHODS:

PROCEDURES:

GRAPHS OR TABLES

SUMMARY:

CALCULATIONS

FORMULAS

TITLE	BOOK No.	DATE
NAME	PROJECT No.	FROM PAGE No.

SIGNATURE	DATE	WITNESS/INSTRUCTOR	DATE

Date: _____

TITLE:

INTRODUCTION:

MATERIALS AND METHODS:

PROCEDURES:

GRAPHS OR TABLES

SUMMARY:

CALCULATIONS

FORMULAS

TITLE		BOOK No.	DATE
NAME		PROJECT No.	FROM PAGE No.

SIGNATURE	DATE	WITNESS/INSTRUCTOR	DATE

Date: _____

TITLE:

INTRODUCTION:

MATERIALS AND METHODS:

PROCEDURES:

GRAPHS OR TABLES

SUMMARY:

CALCULATIONS

FORMULAS

TITLE	BOOK No.	DATE
NAME	PROJECT No.	FROM PAGE No.

SIGNATURE	DATE	WITNESS/INSTRUCTOR	DATE

Date: _____

TITLE:

INTRODUCTION:

MATERIALS AND METHODS:

PROCEDURES:

GRAPHS OR TABLES

SUMMARY:

CALCULATIONS

FORMULAS

TITLE		BOOK No.	DATE
NAME		PROJECT No.	FROM PAGE No.

SIGNATURE	DATE	WITNESS/INSTRUCTOR	DATE

Date: _____

TITLE:

INTRODUCTION:

MATERIALS AND METHODS:

PROCEDURES:

GRAPHS OR TABLES

SUMMARY:

CALCULATIONS

FORMULAS

TITLE		BOOK No.	DATE
NAME		PROJECT No.	FROM PAGE No.

SIGNATURE	DATE	WITNESS/INSTRUCTOR	DATE

Date: _____

TITLE:

INTRODUCTION:

MATERIALS AND METHODS:

PROCEDURES:

GRAPHS OR TABLES

SUMMARY:

CALCULATIONS

FORMULAS

TITLE	BOOK No.	DATE
NAME	PROJECT No.	FROM PAGE No.

SIGNATURE	DATE	WITNESS/INSTRUCTOR	DATE

Date: _____

TITLE:

INTRODUCTION:

MATERIALS AND METHODS:

PROCEDURES:

GRAPHS OR TABLES

SUMMARY:

CALCULATIONS

FORMULAS

TITLE	BOOK No.	DATE
NAME	PROJECT No.	FROM PAGE No.

SIGNATURE	DATE	WITNESS/INSTRUCTOR	DATE

Date: _____

TITLE:

INTRODUCTION:

MATERIALS AND METHODS:

PROCEDURES:

GRAPHS OR TABLES

SUMMARY:

CALCULATIONS

FORMULAS

TITLE	BOOK No.	DATE
NAME	PROJECT No.	FROM PAGE No.

SIGNATURE	DATE	WITNESS/INSTRUCTOR	DATE

Date: _____

TITLE:

INTRODUCTION:

MATERIALS AND METHODS:

PROCEDURES:

GRAPHS OR TABLES

SUMMARY:

CALCULATIONS

FORMULAS

TITLE		BOOK No.	DATE
NAME		PROJECT No.	FROM PAGE No.

SIGNATURE	DATE	WITNESS/INSTRUCTOR	DATE

Date: _____

TITLE:

INTRODUCTION:

MATERIALS AND METHODS:

PROCEDURES:

GRAPHS OR TABLES

SUMMARY:

CALCULATIONS

FORMULAS

TITLE	BOOK No.	DATE
NAME	PROJECT No.	FROM PAGE No.

SIGNATURE	DATE	WITNESS/INSTRUCTOR	DATE

Date: _____

TITLE:

INTRODUCTION:

MATERIALS AND METHODS:

PROCEDURES:

GRAPHS OR TABLES

SUMMARY:

CALCULATIONS

FORMULAS

TITLE		BOOK No.	DATE
NAME		PROJECT No.	FROM PAGE No.

SIGNATURE	DATE	WITNESS/INSTRUCTOR	DATE

Date: _____

TITLE:

INTRODUCTION:

MATERIALS AND METHODS:

PROCEDURES:

GRAPHS OR TABLES

SUMMARY:

CALCULATIONS

FORMULAS

TITLE		BOOK No.	DATE
NAME		PROJECT No.	FROM PAGE No.

SIGNATURE	DATE	WITNESS/INSTRUCTOR	DATE

Date: _____

TITLE:

INTRODUCTION:

MATERIALS AND METHODS:

PROCEDURES:

GRAPHS OR TABLES

SUMMARY:

CALCULATIONS

FORMULAS

Made in the USA
Middletown, DE
12 September 2024